REFLEC
FOR

REFLECTIONS
FOR
LENT

22 February – 7 April 2012

MARTYN PERCY
ANGELA TILBY
JANE WILLIAMS

Church House Publishing
Church House
Great Smith Street
London SW1P 3AZ

ISBN 978 0 7151 4248 6

Published 2011 by Church House Publishing
Copyright © The Archbishops' Council 2011

The opinions expressed in this book are those of the
authors and do not necessarily reflect the official policy of
the General Synod or The Archbishops' Council of the
Church of England.

Designed and typeset by Hugh Hillyard-Parker

Printed and bound by CPI Group (UK) Ltd, Croydon, CR0 4YY

Contents

About the authors

Martyn Percy is Principal of Ripon College Cuddesdon and the Oxford Ministry Course. He is also Professor of Theological Education at King's College London, Professorial Research Fellow at Heythrop College London and an Honorary Canon of Salisbury Cathedral.

Angela Tilby is an Anglican priest in Cambridge and was previously Vice-Principal of Westcott House, Cambridge. Prior to that, she was a senior producer at the BBC, where she made several acclaimed television programmes and series. She continues to combine parish ministry with her work as a freelance television producer, writer and broadcaster.

Jane Williams Jane Williams lectures at St Mellitus College, London and Chelmsford, and is a visiting lecturer at King's College London. She taught previously at Trinity Theological College, Bristol.

About *Reflections for Lent*

Based on the *Common Worship Lectionary* readings for Morning Prayer, these daily reflections are is designed to enhance your spiritual journey though the forty days from Ash Wednesday to Holy Saturday. The aim is to provide rich, contemporary and engaging insights into Scripture, refreshing and inspiring times of personal prayer.

Each page lists the lectionary readings for the day, with the main psalms for that day highlighted in **bold**. The Collect of the day – either the *Common Worship* collect or the shorter additional collect – is also included.

For those using this book in conjunction with a service of Morning Prayer, the following conventions apply: a psalm printed in parentheses is omitted if it has been used as the opening canticle at that office; a psalm marked with an asterisk may be shortened if desired.

A short reflection is provided on either the Old or New Testament reading. The reflections have been written by three highly respected Christian authors, all bringing their own emphases, enthusiasms and approaches to biblical interpretation to bear.

Regular users of Morning Prayer and *Time to Pray* (from *Common Worship: Daily Prayer*) and anyone who follows the lectionary for their regular Bible reading will benefit from the rich variety of traditions represented in these stimulating and accessible pieces.

If you would like to continue the pattern of daily reading and reflection in this book beyond Lent, an annual volume of *Reflections for Daily Prayer* is also available. Please see the back page of this book for more details.

Wednesday 22 February

Ash Wednesday

Daniel 9.3-6, 17-19

'... we have sinned and done wrong' (v.5)

No one likes to talk about sin; it is guilt-inducing, moralizing and anti-social to do so. Yet we ignore the concept at our peril. For we run risks of propagating general, vague morality, yet rooted in little that might offset this – moral, but no compass?

Moreover, we already know enough about our children to have grasped that acquisition has replaced aspiration; vocation given way to fulfilment. Children know what they want to have, but not what they want to be. Their heroes are no longer persons with exemplary lifestyles, but are rather individuals with conspicuous material excess.

Are we part of that generation that aspires to wealth, but not necessarily to goodness? The 'grammar of sin', or rather its absence, is a real issue for our society. And it is a more subtle problem than one might suppose. Look how easily our vapid consumerism, for example, has undermined discipline, patience and charity.

So today's uncompromising text from Daniel is a wake-up call. It is a reminder that we all stand before God and will be judged. Not on what we have amassed, but on the content, quality and character of our lives. We will be weighed – and found wanting.

The good news is that God is ready to receive all who turn to him. He is waiting. As the mystics say, God has only one weakness – his heart. It is too soft. And as Lent begins today, we turn to that heart, and away from all that keeps us from becoming the people that God intended us to be.

COLLECT

Almighty and everlasting God,
you hate nothing that you have made
and forgive the sins of all those who are penitent:
create and make in us new and contrite hearts
that we, worthily lamenting our sins
and acknowledging our wretchedness,
may receive from you, the God of all mercy,
perfect remission and forgiveness;
through Jesus Christ your Son our Lord,
who is alive and reigns with you,
in the unity of the Holy Spirit,
one God, now and for ever.

Psalms **77** *or* **78.1-39***
Genesis 39
Galatians 2.11-end

Galatians 2.11-end

'... the life I now live in the flesh' (v.20)

Peter and Paul wrestling over the gospel and contending for the truth may seem strange to us today. Yet even now, the Christian faith contains a number of competitive theories as to what its main priorities should be. However, there is a common thread that runs through them all. Out of the ashes of Good Friday, hope and new life are born. And the disciples are to be the ambassadors of the transformation found in the person of Jesus.

The resurrection, in other words, is something that does not draw disciples so much into a new sect, as it does send them out – with joy, conviction, and a desire to serve the world and the needs of others in the name of the living Christ. And this is done in love. It is not a task; it is an entire reconfiguration of one's life. You cannot command people to love. Love is for falling into. It is a state of being, as well as doing.

This does not make living the Christian life together easy, mind. As Paul knows well, the things that inspire us are not the formal rules, regulations and codes that often govern our religion. What motivates and inspires us is faith and love. And, perhaps, especially the example of others: faith 'en-fleshed'. What is set out and lived in the life of others is what can transform us, and make us into better people ourselves. One saint, in his own charge to his community, says: 'go and preach the gospel throughout all the world. If absolutely necessary, use words ...'.

Holy God,
our lives are laid open before you:
rescue us from the chaos of sin
and through the death of your Son
bring us healing and make us whole
in Jesus Christ our Lord.

COLLECT

3

Galatians 3.1-14

'... those who believe are blessed with Abraham who believed' (v.9)

As Christians, how do we learn? Paul argues that the Christian life is not only learned through formulae or law, but also by faith. Christian wisdom, although it is rooted in Scripture and other writings, is also birthed in what we learn through practising our beliefs, and in our life of prayer. It is about walking by faith and not with sight – seeing beyond what can be seen. Paul, in appealing to Abraham, invites us to see that we might learn as much about faith through our practice as in what might be preached to us.

Ultimately, we can only teach people *about* Christianity. People have to discover it for themselves through practice. Christian wisdom is built up through the careful cultivation of reflection, practice and wisdom, with each new day building up a gradual, rich and organic repository of knowledge – stored, living wisdom – that helps us refine our discipleship and ministry as we continue to serve God. We can teach people about Jesus, but it is by faith that he is encountered.

So Paul's appeal to Abraham is no accident. By faith, Abraham stepped out into the unknown with God. By faith, Abraham's nascent belief and trust flourished, and was blessed – and so became a blessing. Paul, in drawing on Abraham, is teaching us about wisdom and the ongoing nature of partaking. Wisdom, then, is more than knowledge. It is more than committing texts, traditions or liturgies to memory. It is about walking in understanding. Moving with God, indeed, before you might know where you are going.

COLLECT

Almighty and everlasting God,
you hate nothing that you have made
and forgive the sins of all those who are penitent:
create and make in us new and contrite hearts
that we, worthily lamenting our sins
and acknowledging our wretchedness,
may receive from you, the God of all mercy,
perfect remission and forgiveness;
through Jesus Christ your Son our Lord,
who is alive and reigns with you,
in the unity of the Holy Spirit,
one God, now and for ever.

Saturday 25 February

Galatians 3.15-22

'... what was promised through faith in Jesus Christ' (v.22)

I have often remarked that if I could not be an Anglican, and had to choose another denomination, I'd be a Quaker. I have my reasons. I think silence is a greatly underestimated quality and virtue. I think that Quakerism also represents one of the more radically inventive and inclusive Christian traditions. I think that Quakers have a decent political and social edge to their gospel. The religion is unfussy, democratic, deeply thoughtful and, above all, deeply spiritual.

I also think of Sydney Carter, a favourite hymn writer, who wrote 'Lord of the Dance' – and set to a tune that is meant to be danced to. I think of the love of simplicity, and sometimes wonder how I have ended up in a denomination where everything is so complicated. Anglicans seem to be unable to avoid making a drama out of a crisis, an issue out of virtually every occurrence.

It was Bill Vanstone who once remarked that the Church of England is like a swimming pool – all the noise comes from the shallow end. It's true, isn't it? On issues of major gravity, all the noise comes from the shrill reactionary voices that grab the headlines. The voices from the deep are seldom heard – the real words we need to hear are drowned out by the splashing and the shouting.

Yet they are here today in Paul's words: covenant, mediator, promise and seed ('offspring'). The gospel is simple. But it takes a lifetime to understand what it is saying to us about being together as many, yet one, and as sinners, yet redeemed. Paul's appeal, then, is a simple one. Look to Christ, and life, in all its complexities, will fall into perspective.

Holy God,
our lives are laid open before you:
rescue us from the chaos of sin
and through the death of your Son
bring us healing and make us whole
in Jesus Christ our Lord.

COLLECT

Psalms 10, **11** *or* **80**, 82
Genesis 41.25-45
Galatians 3.23 – 4.7

Galatians 3.23 – 4.7

'... so that we might receive adoption as children' (4.5)

We turn today to one of the more extraordinary sequence of passages that we find in the entire New Testament. Paul boldly proclaims the radical inclusiveness of God, and tells us that in Christ, there are no divisions – by race, tribe, gender, class or heritage. In God's kingdom, we are all heirs, children of the same heavenly father. Adopted.

Some years ago, I sat on a local adoption panel, assessing the needs of children and what the adults or parents have to offer. Many of the children placed come from backgrounds of abuse – physical, sexual or other. Others come stigmatized with the knowledge that the 'stock' they have come from is no good. Their parents were no good, so they'll be no good. Yet the process of adoption for some, in a very real sense, is a kind of being born again. No, you don't get back into the womb. What you do get, though, is an affirmation that nurture is far more important than nature: we make the world we live in – the world does not make us. And the new world that Christians are born into is one of equality and one without false divisions.

For children who are adopted – including myself – this often means a second chance. It is an opportunity to become part of an entirely different family – to become part of a new community with different values and possibilities. What matters when we are adopted by God is not what has been, but what will be, and what is to come. To all Christians, Paul simply says that outsiders who receive Christ are now adopted into God's family, irrespective of their roots. And if a son or daughter of God, then they are also heirs.

COLLECT

Almighty God,
whose Son Jesus Christ fasted forty days in the wilderness,
and was tempted as we are, yet without sin:
give us grace to discipline ourselves in obedience to your Spirit;
and, as you know our weakness,
so may we know your power to save;
through Jesus Christ your Son our Lord,
who is alive and reigns with you,
in the unity of the Holy Spirit,
one God, now and for ever.

Psalms **44** *or* 87, **89.1-18**
Genesis 41.46 – 42.5
Galatians 4.8-20

Galatians 4.8-20

'I am again in the pain of childbirth until Christ is formed in you' (v.19)

There is more to Paul's notion of our adoption into the life of God than meets the eye. We are to be born again, by the Spirit – gradually recreated in the image of God. This is more than mere conversion. It is about Christ being 'formed' in us, which in turn says something profound about our humanity. We are all more than the sum of our parts, and to know this and live this is to live in the life of Christ. We are not to regard ourselves as mere keepers of rituals and traditions – or merely to be descended from a religious lineage. We are part of the dynamic life of God and are to be born again. For Christ to be formed in us is truly to realize our human nature, which in turn is to realize its divine authorship.

Paul's vision of faith, therefore, is one that is rooted in a dynamic appreciation and practice of knowing God, and of Christ being formed in us. This means that our lives, moral character, outlook, lifestyle and relationships will all be transformed by God growing into our lives, just as we grow into God.

This rich image of gestation, maturity and development is at the heart of all spiritual formation. The Christian life is not a set of principles that can be quickly learnt and swotted up on, and the exam then passed. It is a life of growth, pruning, development, commitment, wisdom, maturity, chastening and encouragement. It is, in short, learning and growing through a living relationship.

Heavenly Father,
your Son battled with the powers of darkness,
and grew closer to you in the desert:
help us to use these days to grow in wisdom and prayer
that we may witness to your saving love
in Jesus Christ our Lord.

COLLECT

7

Wednesday 29 February

Psalms **6**, 17 *or* **119.105-128**
Genesis 42.6-17
Galatians 4.21 – 5.1

Galatians 4.21 – 5.1

'For freedom Christ has set us free' (5.1)

Paul's somewhat playful (yet serious) excursions into nature and nurture, birth, adoption and lineage, continue in today's reading. Thomas Fuller, a seventeenth-century Anglican priest, expressed it like this:

> 'Lord, I find the genealogy of my Saviour strangely chequered, with four remarkable changes in four generations:
> Rehoboam begat Abijah: (A bad father begat a bad son)
> Abijah begat Asa: (A bad father and a good son)
> Asa begat Jehoshaphat: (A good father and a good son)
> Jehoshaphat begat Jehorom: (A good father and a bad son).

> I see Lord, from hence, that my Father's piety cannot be handed on: That is bad news for me. I see also that actual impiety is not hereditary; that is good news for my son!'

Many biblical commentators have pointed out that the genealogy of Jesus is full of some surprising and rather suspect stock. There are some people lurking in Jesus' 'family tree' that do not augur well for the future. Paul is saying, very plainly, that our status as children of God does not rest on our pasts, but on how we live our Christian lives now, in the light of the freedom and the promises God has bestowed upon us.

Many people today are interested in finding out more about their ancestors. But Paul wants us to think about our descendants. Having the 'faith of our fathers' is simply not enough. It must be embodied in the here and now. Good and evil were part of Christ's own ancestry. Paul is reminding us that God's grace does not run in the blood.

COLLECT

Almighty God,
whose Son Jesus Christ fasted forty days in the wilderness,
and was tempted as we are, yet without sin:
give us grace to discipline ourselves in obedience to your Spirit;
and, as you know our weakness,
so may we know your power to save;
through Jesus Christ your Son our Lord,
who is alive and reigns with you,
in the unity of the Holy Spirit,
one God, now and for ever.

Psalms **42**, 43 *or* 90, **92**
Genesis 42.18-28
Galatians 5.2-15

Galatians 5.2-15

'A little yeast leavens the whole batch of dough' (v.9)

My favourite Christmas cracker joke is: 'Why did the mushroom go to the party?' Answer: 'Because he was a fun guy'. So, in apparently one of his more innocent phrases, Paul tells us most of what we probably need to know about our discipleship: yeast.

Yeast? That microbe fungus? That discardable and forgettable material that is, oddly, the key to so much of our lives? For yeast is what ferments the wine and beer. It makes the dough rise to make the bread. It is the tiny, insignificant catalyst for our basic commodities and the formation of our communities. The leaven in the lump; the difference between bread and dough; juice and wine; refreshment and celebration.

Paul seldom quotes Jesus in his writings. But, in today's passage, the reference to yeast, and to loving one another, have clear echoes of the gospels that Paul will have known. And here he uses it to teach the Galatians about how to be the Church. Not divided over circumcision or un-circumcision – but united by 'faith working through love'.

The yeast, then, is an idea about how to be together in the world and the Church. For yeast, to fulfil its function is ultimately to be lost and dispersed into the higher purposes to which it is given. Paul, like Jesus, invites us to lose ourselves in something much bigger. But not pointlessly. Rather, in dying to our context, we activate it. We become the catalyst that brings flavour, strength, depth, potency and growth. Without yeast, there is no loaf, just dough. Literally, we die to ourselves for growth. We are the ingredient that helps to make bread for the world.

Heavenly Father,
your Son battled with the powers of darkness,
and grew closer to you in the desert:
help us to use these days to grow in wisdom and prayer
that we may witness to your saving love
in Jesus Christ our Lord.

COLLECT

Lent

Friday 2 March

Psalms **22** *or* **88** (95)
Genesis 42.29-end
Galatians 5.16-end

Galatians 5.16-end

'... the fruit of the Spirit' (v.22)

It is possible to characterize Paul's categorizations according to speed. Put simply, the 'lusts of the flesh' are about quick results, instant gratification, shortcuts, the instant sating of desire. The 'fruit of the Spirit', on the other hand, does not grow overnight. It takes time. The cultivation of joy, peace, patience, kindness, self-control, humility, gentleness and faithfulness take a lifetime. A lifetime, indeed, of wisdom, maturity, practice, humility and learning. Love that is worthy of the name may begin with a spark, but it never comes fully formed. Like a person, there is much growing to be reckoned with.

Paul's lists, then, take on a fascinating dimension: time. Anger, immorality, envy – you name it – well up in an instant. But they also quickly subside. Yet we can often spend the rest of our lives living with the results. Paul, in listing the fruits of the spirit – and comparing them to the 'fruits of the flesh' – is offering a careful and considered judgement about the Church as a community of patience and forbearance. In an age when decisions and clarity are so sought after, it is sometimes sobering to be reminded of the call to be patient and kind; to have self-control; and perhaps, who knows, to be gentle with one another, even if that means living with uncertainty and a lack of consensus.

So, let God set the pace; the bread rises in time; the wine matures only when it is ready; God's fruit takes time to come of age. It is almost as though Paul is saying to the Church: reach – but do not grasp. Hold – but do not clutch. Embrace – but do not smother. Strive – yet be patient. Hope – yet let it be. Love – yet surrender all to God. Pray purposefully – and be at peace.

COLLECT

Almighty God,
whose Son Jesus Christ fasted forty days in the wilderness,
and was tempted as we are, yet without sin:
give us grace to discipline ourselves in obedience to your Spirit;
and, as you know our weakness,
so may we know your power to save;
through Jesus Christ your Son our Lord,
who is alive and reigns with you,
in the unity of the Holy Spirit,
one God, now and for ever.

10

Psalms 59, **63** *or* 96, **97**, 100
Genesis 43.1-15
Galatians 6

Galatians 6

'... for you reap whatever you sow' (v. 7)

'Reap what you sow' is one of the more resonant biblical mantras – one that has found its way into Pentecostal hymnody, as well as many a sermon. At the heart of the phrase is a simple idea, one that echoes a frequently occurring theme of the Old Testament – the 'parents have eaten sour grapes ... and the children's teeth are set on edge'.

A society that puts work, pleasure and money at the heart of its priorities will raise a generation of individualistic, distracted and avaricious children. The development of moral character and social awareness will, alas, be secondary. Paul tells us to beware of this in the Church and in the world. Churches can foster and focus distinctive values that provide leaven in complex contexts. So faith communities often find themselves promoting forms of goodness that secular organizations might miss.

Through a simple ministry of attentiveness, hospitality, care and celebration, churches sometimes do more good for their communities than they can often know. Churches may simply offer regular lunches to the needy, or open house for tea and coffee at any time – the potency of the practice lies in the latency, and is significant. These practices say something about the possibilities for different kinds of space and time in the world – social, pastoral, spiritual. They open up a different side of the Church to the world.

The Church, in other words, is an extension of Christ's love for the world, and helps to inaugurate that new creation that is rooted in grace and hope. So, let us sow the seeds of Christ's love, patience and gentleness where we can, for the harvest reaped will come of such faith.

Heavenly Father,
your Son battled with the powers of darkness,
and grew closer to you in the desert:
help us to use these days to grow in wisdom and prayer
that we may witness to your saving love
in Jesus Christ our Lord.

COLLECT

11

Monday 5 March

Psalms 26, **32** *or* **98**, 99, 101
Genesis 43.16-end
Hebrews 1

Hebrews 1

'... he has spoken to us by a Son' (v.2)

There is no prologue or introduction to Hebrews, no greeting to those for whom the letter is intended and no named author. In making the point that God is the one who speaks, the writer simply edits himself out, allowing his message to burst upon us from the very first verse.

The message is majestic in its simplicity and scope. God spoke through the prophets to our ancestors. This means that God has always been a communicating God. He has spoken through the prophets to our ancestors in faith. But now, in these 'last days', God has spoken to us in a more intimate way, by a Son. This inaugurates a new level of God's engagement with us.

Like most people in the ancient world, those who received this letter believed in invisible powers, both evil and good. Through a skilfully crafted medley of texts, mostly from the psalms, the writer sets out to prove that the authority of the Son is final. He is not a mere angel, but a Son. He not only conveys God's will; he is the imprint of his being.

As we continue through Lent, Hebrews challenges us afresh to put God first, to listen to his voice and today, as every day, to seek his reflection in the face of Christ.

COLLECT

Almighty God,
you show to those who are in error the light of your truth,
that they may return to the way of righteousness:
grant to all those who are admitted
    into the fellowship of Christ's religion,
that they may reject those things
    that are contrary to their profession,
and follow all such things as are agreeable to the same;
through our Lord Jesus Christ,
who is alive and reigns with you,
in the unity of the Holy Spirit,
one God, now and for ever.

Hebrews 2.1-9

'Jesus ... crowned with glory and honour ' (v.9)

It is easy to drift away from Christian faith. Those who received this letter were tempted to neglect their salvation and so, sometimes, are we. The writer calls us back to fundamentals. God is consistent. In the past, his message was delivered through intermediaries, and its validity was proved by the stern fact that disobedience resulted in judgement.

The salvation offered now is of a different order. In Christ, God has revealed in a new way his commitment to humanity. The author quotes the eighth psalm, a wonderful hymn of praise for the miracle of creation. God has a royal destiny in mind for human beings. We were created beneath the angels, but God's intention has always been that we should fulfil the destiny of Adam by becoming wise and gentle princes of paradise.

In the here and now, we do not fulfil this great promise. Like the Hebrews of the letter, we are easily discouraged from our destiny by suffering and temptation. What makes transformation possible is Jesus Christ. He, too, was made lower than the angels, but he has now fulfilled Adam's vocation and is indeed 'crowned with glory and honour'.

But this triumph has not been without cost. It is not in spite of, but because of, his suffering and death. What does this say to us about the cost of discipleship?

Almighty God,
by the prayer and discipline of Lent
may we enter into the mystery of Christ's sufferings,
and by following in his Way
come to share in his glory;
through Jesus Christ our Lord.

COLLECT

Wednesday 7 March

Hebrews 2.10-end

'... the pioneer of their salvation' (v.10)

God's purpose is to bring 'many children to glory'. We are called to share in the family likeness of Jesus Christ.

The author of Hebrews urges us to contemplate the coronation of Jesus, recognizing that it is the consequence of his willingness to share our humanity to the very end, to death itself. Hebrews is noted for its stress on the humanity of Christ. Christ shares our condition, we are his brothers and sisters. This is why the author describes him as the 'pioneer' of salvation, the one who goes ahead and marks the way so that we can follow. We can trust him as our pace-setter in the race of life. As long as we keep focused on him, we will keep going towards the goal. When we lose heart, we need to recall what he has achieved for us by sharing our flesh and blood. He has made us holy, liberating us from the fear of death and so destroying the hold that death has over us.

At this point, the author introduces another image to help us understand what Christ can mean to us. His mediating role is a priestly role; he offers the sacrifice that sets us free. As a faithful priest, he knows what it is to be tested and tempted. His encouragement to us comes from his own experience.

COLLECT

Almighty God,
you show to those who are in error the light of your truth,
that they may return to the way of righteousness:
grant to all those who are admitted
    into the fellowship of Christ's religion,
that they may reject those things
    that are contrary to their profession,
and follow all such things as are agreeable to the same;
through our Lord Jesus Christ,
who is alive and reigns with you,
in the unity of the Holy Spirit,
one God, now and for ever.

Psalms **34** *or* 113, **115**
Genesis 45.1-15
Hebrews 3.1-6

Thursday 8 March

Hebrews 3.1-6

'... we are his house' (v.6)

The author's purpose is to strengthen faith, to help those who were wavering to find stability and confidence. He does this by explaining that they are already 'partners' in a high calling; they are already brothers and sisters of the Son; they are already holy after the pattern of Jesus the 'high priest of our confession'. We begin from the fact of our Christian calling, the reality that we are marked with the cross of Christ and called to fulfil a royal destiny.

The author now introduces another theme that runs through the letter, that of the house of God, the temple. The temple is the place where God meets his people. But he is not thinking about the earthly temple in Jerusalem; Hebrews was almost certainly written after its destruction. What he is doing is tracing a pattern. Just as Moses was faithful 'in God's house' (even before the earthly temple was built), so Jesus is faithful, and even more to be trusted since he is not only God's apostle and high priest, but also his Son. His faithfulness to his vocation is not only an example for us, it provides our ultimate security. Our Christian calling is to become God's house, a place where all creation meets with God and finds its hope and its salvation.

Almighty God,
by the prayer and discipline of Lent
may we enter into the mystery of Christ's sufferings,
and by following in his Way
come to share in his glory;
through Jesus Christ our Lord.

COLLECT

Lent

Psalms 40, **41** *or* **139**
Genesis 45.16-end
Hebrews 3.7-end

Hebrews 3.7-end

'... do not harden your hearts' (v.8)

Hebrews does not only encourage; there is a note of warning that runs through the whole letter. This can sound unattractively threatening to us, but the author is simply reminding us of the experience of God's people as told in Scripture. The repeated quotation from Psalm 95 recalls the failure of God's people to trust him in the wilderness. They 'went astray in their hearts', they turned away from the living God, and it was because of their loss of confidence that they were unable to enter the Promised Land. The unbelief that the author refers to here is not the honest doubt that accompanies many faithful Christians. It is rather a gradual hardening of the heart, an attitude of reservation towards the faith that corrodes the will and turns us into half-hearted Christians, hugging our spiritual apathy to ourselves and becoming cynical in our attitudes.

Such spineless faith can deceive ourselves and others. So today, do not abandon your first love (Revelation 2.4), but hold on to the confidence that we have all been given in Christ. Try encouraging someone else (v.13) if you are feeling discouraged. Or take your rebellious thoughts to the great high priest in prayer and ask for his healing. You may find more sorrow and love in your heart than you expected.

COLLECT

Almighty God,
you show to those who are in error the light of your truth,
that they may return to the way of righteousness:
grant to all those who are admitted
    into the fellowship of Christ's religion,
that they may reject those things
    that are contrary to their profession,
and follow all such things as are agreeable to the same;
through our Lord Jesus Christ,
who is alive and reigns with you,
in the unity of the Holy Spirit,
one God, now and for ever.

Hebrews 4.1-13

'... a sabbath rest ... for the people of God' (v.9)

Today's reading continues with the warnings of scripture that it is possible to miss the grace of God, to lose out on his promises. This is an uncomfortable, but perhaps salutary, theme for us to reflect on.

God calls us to stability, to share with Christ in being his 'house' (Hebrews 3.6). This stability is described as 'rest', which is not a description of inactivity, but rather of spiritual focus. We are to be active contemplatives, grounded in the 'sabbath' rest that is the fruit of worship and mirrors God's magnificent 'rest' at the end of creation.

We cannot benefit from that rest unless we really want it. We can never enjoy it until we learn to trust. Today is the day of opportunity. There is an urgency about our response. That is not to say that we are saved by our activism, but God does expect us to make an effort. We are called to examine ourselves in the light of God's word, aware of its power to reveal the truth of our hearts, to help us to see what we really desire and to draw us closer to the rest that God desires for us. For he is the one 'to whom all hearts are open, all desires known and from whom no secrets are hidden'.

Almighty God,
by the prayer and discipline of Lent
may we enter into the mystery of Christ's sufferings,
and by following in his Way
come to share in his glory;
through Jesus Christ our Lord.

COLLECT

Monday 12 March

Hebrews 4.14 – 5.10

'... he learned obedience through what he suffered' (5.8)

The writer to the Hebrews begins today's passage with a bold assertion. Christ is the great high priest whose inner sanctuary is heaven itself. Jesus is like any priest in that his personal sufferings are part of his offering to God. He prays for himself and for others, he deals gently with those who are struggling because he is aware of his own weakness. He has been through the same trials and temptations as we have, and yet, unlike us, he has not fallen short. All this should give us the ultimate confidence to trust him as we approach God with our particular needs.

Yet we misunderstand our great high priest if we assume his obedience was effortless. Even as the Son of God, he needed the discipline of prayer. He was not spared the dilemmas and ambiguities that test us every day. His human life, like ours, was a pilgrimage towards God's perfection. It is because he has persevered to the end that he manifests the eternal priesthood attributed here to Melchizedek.

The fourth-century theologian Gregory of Nazianzus insisted on the reality of Christ's humanity with the statement, 'That which he has not assumed he has not healed'. Our salvation depends not only on Christ's divine Sonship, but on the authenticity of his human struggle.

COLLECT

Almighty God,
whose most dear Son went not up to joy but first he
        suffered pain,
and entered not into glory before he was crucified:
mercifully grant that we, walking in the way of the cross,
may find it none other than the way of life and peace;
through Jesus Christ your Son our Lord,
who is alive and reigns with you,
in the unity of the Holy Spirit,
one God, now and for ever.

Psalms 6, **9** *or* **132**, 133
Genesis 47.28 – end of 48
Hebrews 5.11 – 6.12

Hebrews 5.11 – 6.12

'... on towards perfection' (6.1)

In spite of the promises of God, the progress of the 'Hebrews' has proved disappointing. They have been taught the basics of the Christian faith, but, somehow, they have failed to build on them and are now in danger of falling away altogether. If they are unable to pull themselves together, there is a point at which they may find they have drifted beyond repentance.

This is a worrying suggestion and it is one of the reasons why there were doubts in the early Church about whether Hebrews should be regarded as genuine Scripture. But the point we should attend to is that a familiarity with the mysteries of salvation – along with a stubborn refusal to take them seriously – constitutes a toxic mixture that eventually erodes our capacity to respond to God at all. Grace is given once and for all and, if we have 'tasted the heavenly gift, and have shared in the Holy Spirit', we cannot give it back. Sluggish, half-hearted Christians bring the name of Christ into contempt and so, in the writer's vivid phrase, 'crucify again the Son of God'. This severe judgement is tempered when he recalls the fact that the Hebrews are showing evidence of Christian love in 'serving the saints'. Their situation may be dire, but it is not hopeless. They are not alone in their struggles. Nor are we.

Eternal God,
give us insight
to discern your will for us,
to give up what harms us,
and to seek the perfection we are promised
in Jesus Christ our Lord.

COLLECT

Wednesday 14 March

Hebrews 6.13-end

'... a sure and steadfast anchor of the soul' (v.19)

'Will your anchor hold in the storm of life?' That old chorus draws inspiration from this passage, where Christian hope is likened to an anchor that not only holds the soul sure and steadfast, but goes with Christ into the heavenly sanctuary to plead our cause before God. The basis of our hope is in the character of God, which is shown first in his promise to Abraham. Abraham, steadfast in the same patient endurance to which we are being called, finally obtained God's promise that he would have an heir. But his faithfulness was tested when God required him to offer Isaac in sacrifice. When he demonstrated his obedience and Isaac was saved, God reinforced his original promise with an oath, swearing by himself (Genesis 22.17) in order to confirm his purpose to Abraham's descendants in faith.

So our hope is based on two unshakeable realities: God's promise and his oath. In ancient Israel, an innocent fugitive could take sanctuary in the temple by seizing the horns of the altar. This practice is what lies behind the image of taking refuge and seizing 'the hope set before us'. Boldness in hope prepares the way for heaven, as long as we keep our eyes fixed on Jesus, our forerunner. So it comes back to us. 'Will your anchor hold ...?'

COLLECT

Almighty God,
whose most dear Son went not up to joy but first he
suffered pain,
and entered not into glory before he was crucified:
mercifully grant that we, walking in the way of the cross,
may find it none other than the way of life and peace;
through Jesus Christ your Son our Lord,
who is alive and reigns with you,
in the unity of the Holy Spirit,
one God, now and for ever.

Psalms **56**, 57 *or* **143**, 146
Genesis 49.33 – 50.end
Hebrews 7.1-10

Hebrews 7.1-10

'... priest for ever' (v.3)

We return today to the theme of Christ's eternal priesthood and the way it is foreshadowed by the mysterious figure of Melchizedek.

Melchizedek was the priest-king of Jerusalem who blessed Abraham after his defeat of four enemy kings (Genesis 14.18-19). Melchizedek is mentioned again in the 'royal' Psalm 110, where the anointed king of Zion is declared to belong to the same eternal order of priesthood as he does. The early Christians interpreted Psalm 110 as a prophecy of Christ, and verses from it are frequently quoted in the Gospels to show how Christ fulfils the promises of Jewish scripture. The point being made in these verses is that, even though in his earthly life Christ did not come from the priestly house of Levi, his priesthood is securely founded and is, in fact, greater than Levi's. This is demonstrated by the fact that, figuratively speaking, Levi offered tithes to Christ's counterpart, Melchizedek, through his ancestor Abraham. This rather tortuous argument is intended to build confidence in the unique vocation of the Son of God to stand before the Father as our great high priest. In this role, he transcends earthly ancestry and tradition. Because he lives for ever, his priestly prayer for us cannot fail.

Eternal God,
give us insight
to discern your will for us,
to give up what harms us,
and to seek the perfection we are promised
in Jesus Christ our Lord.

COLLECT

Friday 16 March

Psalms **22** *or* 142, **144**
Exodus 1.1-14
Hebrews 7.11-end

Hebrews 7.11-end

'... a better hope' (v.19)

The argument for the supreme effectiveness of Christ's priesthood continues as the comparison between the old and the new is developed further. The old Levitical priesthood was inevitably imperfect. Its imperfection actually pointed towards 'another priest', who would be different and better, whose new powers would not be compromised by his having been part of an 'imperfect' priestly family.

The coming of Christ as high priest transforms the law requiring priests to be descended from Levi, because the life he brings is simply indestructible; its validity is proved by its total efficacy. In addition, Christ's priesthood is not ended by death, nor is it weakened by his need to offer sacrifice for his own sins before performing the sacrifices for his people. Christ as high priest simply cannot let us down. He is eternally ready to save us; 'he always lives to make intercession' for us.

The profound invitation of this chapter is to offer our prayer consciously through Christ, to see him in our mind's eye as one who stands before the Father on our behalf, taking with him into God's presence all our needs and fears and failures. He is our guarantee of God's good intent towards us, the ultimate fulfilment of God's promise to visit and redeem his people.

COLLECT

Almighty God,
whose most dear Son went not up to joy but first he
    suffered pain,
and entered not into glory before he was crucified:
mercifully grant that we, walking in the way of the cross,
may find it none other than the way of life and peace;
through Jesus Christ your Son our Lord,
who is alive and reigns with you,
in the unity of the Holy Spirit,
one God, now and for ever.

Psalms **31** *or* **147**
Exodus 1.22 – 2.10
Hebrews 8

Saturday 17 March

Hebrews 8

'... a new covenant' (v.8)

We now come to the heart of the argument about Christ's high priesthood. The Jews of Jesus' time believed that the rituals of the temple imitated the worship of the angels in heaven. The author builds on that belief to establish that the earthly temple, for all its magnificence, was only 'a sketch and shadow of the heavenly sanctuary'. It is no longer needed. Jesus now ministers in the heavenly sanctuary, here described as 'the true tent', a reference back to the tent of meeting in the wilderness. The impermanence of Moses' 'tent' points forward to what is now permanent. Christ's enthronement in heaven has revealed the providential imperfection of the old and abolished it. This does not invalidate Judaism, which, during the early Christian era was radicalizing itself in the wake of the destruction of the Jerusalem temple. But it does point us to the fact that the new covenant is overwhelmingly generous and inclusive.

The ministry of Jesus to us is based on the forgiveness of sins. In the new covenant, God's commandments become intimate to God's people, written on their hearts, as Jeremiah's prophecy foretold. The new covenant is the fruit of Christ's ministry and the glorious message of this chapter is 'we have such a high priest'. There is nothing and no one beyond the reach of his prayer and his compassion.

COLLECT

Eternal God,
give us insight
to discern your will for us,
to give up what harms us,
and to seek the perfection we are promised
in Jesus Christ our Lord.

23

Monday 19 March
Joseph of Nazareth

Isaiah 11.1-10

'... the earth will be full of the knowledge of the Lord' (v.9)

Isaiah prophecies the coming of a descendant of David, a 'shoot from the stock of Jesse', whose kingdom will see the end of violence and a new order being inaugurated based on justice and gentleness. The king will be anointed with the Holy Spirit, and so will be 'Messiah' (the Greek translation of which is 'Christ').

This reading is given for St Joseph's day because Joseph was a distant descendent of David, and it is through Joseph that Jesus is linked to David and to his 'messianic' kingship. We know very little about Joseph other than the brief details at the beginning of the Gospels of Matthew and Luke. What we see of him there suggests that he was a faithful and trustworthy servant of God, the protector of Mary his wife and the baby Jesus, who puts their needs before his own comfort and convenience. He represents those many faithful and trustworthy servants of God whose role in history is unspectacular in terms of fame and glory, but absolutely vital for the kingdom of God.

Joseph is a good role model for us as we continue through Lent, keeping in our minds a vision of the kingdom while being ready to keep to the disciplines of prayer and obedience in the present.

COLLECT

God our Father,
who from the family of your servant David
raised up Joseph the carpenter
to be the guardian of your incarnate Son
and husband of the Blessed Virgin Mary:
give us grace to follow him
in faithful obedience to your commands;
through Jesus Christ your Son our Lord,
who is alive and reigns with you,
in the unity of the Holy Spirit,
one God, now and for ever.

Lent

Psalms 54, **79** *or* **5**, 6 (8)
Exodus 2.23 – 3.20
Hebrews 9.15-end

Tuesday 20 March

Hebrews 9.15-end

'... without the shedding of blood there is no forgiveness of sins' (v.22)

We tend to find the idea of blood-sacrifice repellent, but the sacrificial system was based on a genuine reverence for life. It is because life is the most precious thing of all that it is offered to God. This chapter builds on this ancient assumption but changes it beyond recognition. The new covenant, like the old, is ratified by death and sacrifice, but Christ's death is a once-and-for-all offering of his life, which has the effect of dismantling the whole system. He brings about what the old system could not achieve, the removal of sin.

Christ's sacrifice is unrepeatable. It does not need to be repeated, nor could it be, because Christ, like any other human being, dies only once. The astonishing truth is that his sacrifice is sufficient to deal with the failures and sins and moral compromises of all his people. He has appeared before God on our behalf 'to remove sin by the sacrifice of himself'.

The reference to his second coming (v.28) recalls the reappearance of the high priest from the Holy of Holies on the day of atonement, demonstrating that the sacrifice has been accepted. In the words of the hymn by William Bright:

'"One offering, single and complete",
with lips and hearts we say;
but what he never can repeat
he shows forth day by day.'

Merciful Lord,
absolve your people from their offences,
that through your bountiful goodness
we may all be delivered from the chains of those sins
which by our frailty we have committed;
grant this, heavenly Father,
for Jesus Christ's sake, our blessed Lord and Saviour,
who is alive and reigns with you,
in the unity of the Holy Spirit,
one God, now and for ever.

COLLECT

25

Psalms 63, **90** *or* **119.1-32**
Exodus 4.1-23
Hebrews 10.1-18

Hebrews 10.1-18

'... he sat down at the right hand of God' (v.12)

What Christ achieved for us is final and complete, and this is emphasized by his seated posture. He is no longer standing like a temple priest to offer sacrifice every morning and evening. We live in the time between the victory and the end, waiting and praying that all that remains opposed to him is won over or defeated (compare Hebrews 10.13 with 1.13).

So what should our attitude be in this waiting time? The writer suggests, rather optimistically perhaps, that those who are cleansed once for all will cease to have any consciousness of sin (v.2) and even that we should no longer be in need of forgiveness (v.18). His perspective is that of one who is living in 'the last days'. But for us, this raises different issues. How are we to live in response to the finality of Christ's sacrifice?

The quotation from Psalm 40 suggests an answer. We are not to live in anxiety about whether or not we are acceptable to God. This anxiety might tempt us to try to appease God or bargain with him. But God takes no pleasure in such strategies. Instead, our prayer should be, 'I have come to do your will, O God'. Offering ourselves afresh in God's service is the response to all that Christ has done for us.

COLLECT

Merciful Lord,
absolve your people from their offences,
that through your bountiful goodness
we may all be delivered from the chains of those sins
which by our frailty we have committed;
grant this, heavenly Father,
for Jesus Christ's sake, our blessed Lord and Saviour,
who is alive and reigns with you,
in the unity of the Holy Spirit,
one God, now and for ever.

Thursday 22 March

Hebrews 10.19-25

*'Let us hold fast to the confession of our hope
without wavering' (v.23)*

The keynote of today's reading is confidence. We can throw off anxiety and hesitation and follow Jesus into God's presence, sure that we have direct access to God. This boldness is not primarily a *feeling*. It is more a readiness to rest in the reality of what Christ has made possible. Faith, again, is not a feeling or an intellectual certainty. It is 'holding fast' to the hope that we have been given because 'he who has promised is faithful'.

Great though this confidence is, it is not to make us complacent. Confidence is corporate. We belong to the community of believers, and we should not neglect the habit of coming together in prayer and praise. This is the context in which we are able to build each other up, 'provoking one another to love and good deeds'. The common life of the Church is where we are formed as Christians and learn Christ-like habits of gentleness and virtue. Going to church is not simply a matter of choice. It is an expression of the confidence we have in Christ, a confidence to be seen and counted as Christians. Hope and faith and love increase when they are shared.

Merciful Lord,
you know our struggle to serve you:
when sin spoils our lives
and overshadows our hearts,
come to our aid
and turn us back to you again;
through Jesus Christ our Lord.

COLLECT

27

Friday 23 March

Psalms **102** *or* 17, **19**
Exodus 6.2-13
Hebrews 10.26-end

Hebrews 10.26-end

'It is a fearful thing to fall into the hands of the living God' (v.31)

This is perhaps the hardest passage for reflection from Hebrews, and we cannot help but be aware of the writer's somewhat threatening tone. He tells us of the dangers of continuing in sin after receiving knowledge of the truth, seeming to discount any possibility of a second repentance after conversion. There are Christians today who are haunted by the fear of God's anger, but there are perhaps as many who sit too lightly to the prospect of divine judgement.

We should not 'shrink back' from the challenge of these verses, but use this passage to reflect on what it might mean to us to 'fall into the hands of the living God'.

There is a long tradition that the love and fire of God are the same reality; how we experience them depends on the state of our heart. Christian character is not achieved in a day, and the pains and struggles of Christian life are the crucible in which we are formed to bear the love of God. 'Godly fear' is not the opposite of love, but the proper response of fallible human beings to the beauty and holiness of God. We might feel the fear but we should still go boldly on!

COLLECT

Merciful Lord,
absolve your people from their offences,
that through your bountiful goodness
we may all be delivered from the chains of those sins
which by our frailty we have committed;
grant this, heavenly Father,
for Jesus Christ's sake, our blessed Lord and Saviour,
who is alive and reigns with you,
in the unity of the Holy Spirit,
one God, now and for ever.

Saturday 24 March

Hebrews 11.1-16

'... he has prepared a city for them' (v.16)

To encourage us to persevere, the writer now begins a great roll-call of faith, beginning with Abel and going on to cite some of the most heroic figures of the Old Testament and Jewish tradition. What all these individuals had in common was that they held fast to realities they could neither see nor fully experience. For them, faith meant living with confidence in the invisible realities of God's presence and providence.

What this means is that history is going somewhere, towards the city of God. It also means that our lives are going somewhere, towards the same heavenly city. We can learn from the heroes of the past and imitate them in living more lightly to the present. They realized that the blessings and sufferings of life were provisional, and were content to live as transient 'strangers and foreigners' on the earth.

The source of the contentment was their trust that God was creating a place of permanence and fulfilment beyond this life. We should take this to mean that our life on this earth is a pilgrimage, not a destination. What is important for us is that our desires are formed by the hope of heaven. Home may be a long way off, but the promise is here and now and every day we come a little nearer to glory.

Merciful Lord,
you know our struggle to serve you:
when sin spoils our lives
and overshadows our hearts,
come to our aid
and turn us back to you again;
through Jesus Christ our Lord.

COLLECT

29

Monday 26 March

Annunciation of Our Lord
to the Blessed Virgin Mary

Psalms 111, 113
1 Samuel 2.1-10
Romans 5.12-end

Romans 5.12-end

'... one man's trespass ... one man's act of righteousness' (v.18)

This dense passage has formed part of the argument for the theology of 'original sin'. It seems to say that death and sin found their entrance into the world through the sin of Adam, and that all human beings, ever since, have been enmeshed in the fatal results of Adam's wrong choice, so that our human ability freely to choose between good and evil is now compromised.

There are good and bad theological arguments on this subject, but 'original sin' does seem to have some psychological and social truth to it. People often find themselves almost constrained to do and be less than they wish; and we are all born into webs of damaged and damaging relationships that at least partially dictate our choices.

But this is not the argument that Paul is presenting here in Romans. He does seem to say, in verse 12, that Adam opens up the possibility of sin to all of us, and we greedily and stupidly use our choices, just as Adam did. But, much more importantly, Paul is saying that God in Christ is at work to give us back our freedom. Our human choices lay burdens on all of us, but God's choice sets us free to live with God and each other, and to give and receive relationships as gifts.

As Mary says yes to God, chains begin to crumble.

COLLECT

We beseech you, O Lord,
pour your grace into our hearts,
that as we have known the incarnation of your Son Jesus Christ
    by the message of an angel,
so by his cross and passion
we may be brought to the glory of his resurrection;
through Jesus Christ your Son our Lord,
who is alive and reigns with you,
in the unity of the Holy Spirit,
one God, now and for ever.

Psalms **35**, 123 *or* 32, **36**
Exodus 8.20-end
Hebrews 11.32 – 12.2

Tuesday 27 March

Hebrews 11.32 – 12.2

'... let us run with perseverance the race that is set before us' (12.1)

This passage is part of Hebrews' great exhortation to faith. The author holds up the steadfast endurance of the great heroes of the Jewish people as an example to the Christian readers of the Letter. From Gideon, Samson and David, through to the more recent martyrs of the Maccabean revolt, just a couple of centuries before Christ, God's people have suffered and endured, upheld by their faith. They never assumed that, because things were going badly for them, God was not to be trusted.

Although the author argues that faith is not something visible, tangible, he also says that other people can help to make it real for us. We are 'surrounded by so great a cloud of witnesses' (12.1) who help us to make sense of our own journey of faith.

Passiontide is a sore test of faith, as Jesus moves inexorably towards the cross. We have to ask why this must always be the pattern of God's love in the world. Why must God's people struggle, why must God's Son suffer and die? Hebrews does not give us an answer, but it does give us a way of life, supported by the evidence of thousands of others who have made the choice to trust. Our faith is not just a private hope, but a passionate witness to the reality of the world. We will trust together, for the sake of all.

Most merciful God,
who by the death and resurrection of your Son Jesus Christ
delivered and saved the world:
grant that by faith in him who suffered on the cross
we may triumph in the power of his victory;
through Jesus Christ your Son our Lord,
who is alive and reigns with you,
in the unity of the Holy Spirit,
one God, now and for ever.

COLLECT

Hebrews 12.3-13

*'... he disciplines us for our good, in order that we may share
his holiness' (v.10)*

Today's passage from Hebrews needs to be approached with caution.
Too many bad arguments have been constructed on the basis of a glib
reading of passages like this one, with disastrous theological and
pastoral consequences. It is not true to say that God deliberately inflicts
suffering on people in order to teach them things, any more than it is
true that parents deliberately punish their children and expect that to
be seen as a sign of love.

Instead, the argument of this passage goes something like this: parents
may choose never to allow their children to experience any hardship
or anxiety, but, if they do, they also choose never to allow their children
to grow up and take their place in the adult world.

In our Christian life, we are encouraged to face the reality of a broken
and hurt world, which will break and hurt us, too, just as it did Jesus.
In this world, we can either whine and give up our faith, like children
having a tantrum, or we can grow up, and accept our adult, Christian
role in the world.

Hebrews calls this sharing God's holiness. And that suggests that
holiness is not a life set apart, but a life that shares God's love of the
world, even when times are tough.

COLLECT

Most merciful God,
who by the death and resurrection of your Son Jesus Christ
delivered and saved the world:
grant that by faith in him who suffered on the cross
we may triumph in the power of his victory;
through Jesus Christ your Son our Lord,
who is alive and reigns with you,
in the unity of the Holy Spirit,
one God, now and for ever.

Psalms **40**, 125 *or* **37***
Exodus 9.13-end
Hebrews 12.14-end

Hebrews 12.14-end

'But you have come ... to the city of the living God' (v.22)

There are two different understandings of religion here. One is theatrical: exhilarating and frightening in equal measures. Its essence is an exciting *experience*, with a beginning and an end. It may be a communal experience, but people leave it, awed and shaken, but not fundamentally changed.

The other is religion of daily holiness, whose mirror image is the vision of the heavenly Jerusalem, where the rejoicing hosts of heaven and earth live with God. The practices of this religion are designed to build parallels here and now with what we long for in the future.

So this religion values, above all, those virtues that build trust and fellowship. It abhors above all those vices that cause bitterness, suspicion and division.

These two pictures of religion do not have to be complete alternatives. Hebrews reminds us that our God is indeed a 'consuming fire', real, potent and all-consuming. But this God is not just a source of exciting personal experiences for us, but the God of the whole world. To serve this God is to be drawn out of ourselves, and our own interesting religious urges, into God's purposes for creation. Our faith is not just for us, but to help us build a community that will be at home in 'the city of the living God'.

Gracious Father,
you gave up your Son
out of love for the world:
lead us to ponder the mysteries of his passion,
that we may know eternal peace
through the shedding of our Saviour's blood,
Jesus Christ our Lord.

COLLECT

33

Friday 30 March

Hebrews 13.1-16

'Let mutual love continue' (v. 1)

In the Christian world, everyday life is profound, transparent and porous. There isn't a 'sacred' sphere and a secular one: everyday actions, such as the offering of hospitality, can be a place of divine encounter, filled with light that streams out and illuminates the ordinary, making it supernatural. Nor is there the kind of spirituality or religious observance where an individual can measure their own achievement and progress; instead, the lives of other Christians, their needs and their failures, almost leak into ours: all are bound together, so that the suffering of one is the suffering of all, the success of one is the success of all.

The readers of the Letter to the Hebrews, like the rest of us, obviously found this frustrating at times. It sounds as though they were sometimes tempted to return to a more systematic kind of religious observance, 'inside the camp', where it is clearer what God does and does not have a right to expect of us.

But the writer is adamant that to be with Jesus is the only point of being a Christian. Where he is, we have to be, and we have to be there with the others who have made this choice, whatever we may think of them. This is a love affair, not a system of brownie points.

COLLECT

Most merciful God,
who by the death and resurrection of your Son Jesus Christ
delivered and saved the world:
grant that by faith in him who suffered on the cross
we may triumph in the power of his victory;
through Jesus Christ your Son our Lord,
who is alive and reigns with you,
in the unity of the Holy Spirit,
one God, now and for ever.

Psalms **23**, 127 *or* 41, **42**, 43
Exodus 11
Hebrews 13.17-end

Hebrews 13.17-end

'... may the God of peace ... make you complete in everything good'
(vv.20-21)

There is quite a touching account of the relationship between leaders and the led in today's passage from Hebrews. Although the rather hierarchical way in which it is expressed may sound odd to our ears, there are some interesting assumptions built in. Leaders are accountable for those they lead, and the led need to take some responsibility for the well-being of the leader. Both are working for the same end.

Above all, the way in which this relationship is grounded in prayer makes it clear that these are not structures embedded in any normal understanding of power or status. Instead, the writer and the readers are gifts to one another, given by the generosity of the gift-giving God. The author begs for prayer for himself, and then prays for his readers. Lifting from them any burdens his instructions have laid upon them, the writer gives them back to God. The mighty power of God, at work in Jesus, is liberating and energizing. It takes away the need for self-justification and anxiety, and gives us, in exchange, the certainty that we give God pleasure.

This is not a recipe for complacency, but for joy. This is not about us, but about God at work through Jesus Christ, and about the glory that the Father and the Son offer to one another.

Gracious Father,
you gave up your Son
out of love for the world:
lead us to ponder the mysteries of his passion,
that we may know eternal peace
through the shedding of our Saviour's blood,
Jesus Christ our Lord.

COLLECT

Monday 2 April

Monday of Holy Week

Luke 22.1-23

'Do this in remembrance of me' (v.19)

There are lots of echoes in today's reading from Luke.

First of all, Satan, who has been out of sight since the temptation in the wilderness in chapter 4, returns. Jesus may have resisted him, but Judas cannot. His choice does not change Jesus' fate, but it does change his own. Jesus' enemies don't really need Judas to lead them to Jesus; Judas may feel, at this moment, that he has power over Jesus, but Luke makes it clear, as Jesus gives instructions for the Passover meal, that Jesus is still in charge.

Next, as Jesus shares the meal with his followers in a house that is not his own, the echo leads us back to the manger where he was born. That didn't belong to him, either. The one who gives everything owns nothing.

Luke's readers would have recognized this supper in a large room that belonged to a well-off friend. It would have been exactly like the place where, week by week, they shared the Eucharist, repeating Jesus' words, breaking the bread together, guests of one of the better-off Christians, but all equal, nourished by the body and blood.

The words of Jesus at this supper echo through all Christian history, all of us called to this table together, all of us receiving what we have not earned and could not buy, but are given by the generosity of God.

COLLECT

Almighty and everlasting God,
who in your tender love towards the human race
    sent your Son our Saviour Jesus Christ
to take upon him our flesh
and to suffer death upon the cross:
grant that we may follow the example of his patience and
    humility,
and also be made partakers of his resurrection;
through Jesus Christ your Son our Lord,
who is alive and reigns with you,
in the unity of the Holy Spirit,
one God, now and for ever.

Psalm 27
Lamentations 3.1-18
Luke 22.[24-38] 39-53

Tuesday of Holy Week

Luke 22.[24-38] 39-53

'But this is your hour, and the power of darkness!' (v.53)

At the Last Supper, Jesus has woven his disciples together as indissolubly as words and symbols can, and provided for them out of his own sacrificial bounty. But it is clear that, while the disciples can receive, they cannot yet take responsibility for these symbols themselves. They still need to be taught about servant-leadership, and they still do not understand the cost of it.

And so Jesus prays alone in the garden, with his satiated disciples sleeping around him, unaware that soon it will be their turn to be self-giving leaders. When their time came, they would remember Jesus' bitter struggle in the garden and know that doubt and fear are not forbidden for a disciple of Christ. The leadership that Jesus called them to did not need to come effortlessly, with perfect clarity about God's call and its outcome.

Judas presumably thought he was about to exercise decisive leadership. But he was almost laughably superfluous at the one moment when he thought he was going to be in control. Only Jesus pays any attention to him, and then he is lost in the struggle between Jesus' followers and his enemies.

There are profound and unpalatable thoughts about power in today's reading, as there are throughout Holy Week. Those who think they exercise power cannot see the mighty act of God in Jesus, as he walks towards his death.

True and humble king,
hailed by the crowd as Messiah:
grant us the faith to know you and love you,
that we may be found beside you
on the way of the cross,
which is the path of glory.

COLLECT

37

Wednesday 4 April

Wednesday of Holy Week

Psalm 102 [*or* 102.1-18]
Wisdom 1.16 – 2.1; 2.12–22
or Jeremiah 11.18-20
Luke 22.54-end

Luke 22.54-end

'... he went out and wept bitterly' (v.62)

Luke's readers know all about Peter. He was a famous leader of the Church; all the stories about Jesus contain references to Peter, and so do all the stories of the earliest Christian community. They know that Peter was one of the first to recognize God's invitation to gentile Christians, like themselves, and they know that he was martyred for his faith. But they also know this story, told wherever Peter goes. They know it, paradoxically, as the thing that validates Peter's claim to authority, just as they know Paul's story as a persecutor of the faith as part of his passport to Christian leadership. Deep in the heart of the Christian story is a suspicion of Christians who believe they have earned their faith by their own merit, rather than by the free forgiveness of Jesus.

For Christians, there is no shame in failure. The only shame is in not being prepared to accept forgiveness. That is Judas' shame. 'What if' is always a dangerous question, but Jesus predicts that both Judas and Peter will betray him. If Peter can be forgiven, could Judas have been forgiven, too, if he had been brave enough, humble enough, to wait to find out?

Peter sets off, stupidly, believing he will be brave. He steps after Jesus and into his own future, while Judas slinks away to die.

COLLECT

Almighty and everlasting God,
who in your tender love towards the human race
     sent your Son our Saviour Jesus Christ
to take upon him our flesh
and to suffer death upon the cross:
grant that we may follow the example of his patience and
     humility,
and also be made partakers of his resurrection;
through Jesus Christ your Son our Lord,
who is alive and reigns with you,
in the unity of the Holy Spirit,
one God, now and for ever.

Psalms 42, 43
Leviticus 16.2-24
Luke 23.1-25

Luke 23.1-25

'So Pilate gave his verdict' (v.24)

For Pilate, this is just one more in a series of trials that he had to conduct, one more attempt to keep the peace among these quarrelsome people he was trying to govern on behalf of Rome. Pilate did his job efficiently, hearing the evidence and weighing it correctly as worthless. Luke's readers know very well that these charges are unfounded: Jesus did not advocate withholding taxes and did not claim publicly to be the Messiah. These were traps that his enemies had laid for him, but which he had adroitly side-stepped.

So Pilate would, ideally, like to discharge Jesus. He seizes instantly on the hint that Jesus should be in Herod's jurisdiction, rather than his own, but the buck cannot be passed for long. Ultimately, Pilate judges that peace is more important than justice.

Pilate, Herod and the enemies of Jesus assume that the trial and execution will be the end of the matter. But Luke's readers see the undercurrents. They see reconciliation between Pilate and Herod, brought about by Jesus. They see a criminal going free, because of Jesus, and know how many other sinners have been freed by this death. They hear the irony of the fact that the man is called 'Barabbas' – 'son of the father', when the true Son of the Father is going to death so that we may all become children of God.

God our Father,
you have invited us to share in the supper
which your Son gave to his Church
to proclaim his death until he comes:
may he nourish us by his presence,
and unite us in his love;
who is alive and reigns with you,
in the unity of the Holy Spirit,
one God, now and for ever.

COLLECT

Friday 6 April

Good Friday

Hebrews 10.1-10

'I have come to do your will' (v.7)

The prophets and psalmists of the Hebrew Scriptures have already begun to sow the seed of the knowledge that animal sacrifice is not really what God is interested in. These kinds of sacrifice are attempts to placate God, almost to divert God's attention from the behaviour they are trying to atone for. They acknowledge the problem, but refuse to see that the solution cannot be applied externally. What the sacrifices do not do is to change the hearts and wills of the people who offer them. But that is what God longs for.

The quotation from Psalm 40 makes the point: Jesus has come to do God's will.

And so everything changes today. Now, we know that what God offers is a relationship in which we can work with God, knowing him intimately, being part of his purposes for the world. We can't hide behind rituals and ceremonies any more; God has come close, to know and be known.

If that is frighteningly open-ended, it is also liberating. We no longer have to worry about whether our sacrifice has 'worked' to keep God satisfied, because no more sacrifices are required. All that is asked of us is that we come to God, in the company of Jesus, and say the words that he has taught us, 'I have come to do your will'.

COLLECT

Almighty Father,
look with mercy on this your family
for which our Lord Jesus Christ was content to be betrayed
    and given up into the hands of sinners
    and to suffer death upon the cross;
who is alive and glorified with you and the Holy Spirit,
one God, now and for ever.

Psalm 142
Hosea 6.1-6
John 2.18-22

John 2.18-22

'What sign can you show us ...?' (v.18)

During his ministry, Jesus is quite often asked for a 'sign'. The Gospels unanimously testify to Jesus' powers, primarily as a healer, but also as a miracle-worker. And yet people went on asking for a 'sign', and found that nothing they saw or heard was really convincing.

So what could really have worked for these people and the many, many others like them? What would finally convince?

The simple answer is that nothing God does is so plain that we have no choice about recognizing it. Even the resurrection can be doubted. God is extraordinarily uncoercive. Even the mightiest act will not function as a 'sign' unless we have already begun to see the character of the God to whom it bears witness.

God's greatest act is to become human, to live and to die. This ought not to be possible for 'God', on any normal definition of the word. Yet this is what God chooses to do, the mightiest sign of all, a sign of God's commitment, God's willingness to be present to us in all circumstances, God's power to transform without force but with utter creativity.

So the resurrection is a sign of the power of our God, who cannot be forced to abandon us, and whose life is unquenchable. Is that a sign? Only if this is the kind of God we long for.

COLLECT

Grant, Lord,
that we who are baptized into the death
of your Son our Saviour Jesus Christ
may continually put to death our evil desires
and be buried with him;
and that through the grave and gate of death
we may pass to our joyful resurrection;
through his merits,
who died and was buried and rose again for us,
your Son Jesus Christ our Lord.